MCR

COOL GRAVITY ACTIVITIES

Fun Science Projects about Balance

James Hopwood

ABDO
Publishing Company

TO ADULT HELPERS

You're invited to assist an up-and-coming scientist! And it will pay off in many ways. Your children can develop new skills, gain confidence, and do some interesting projects while learning about science. What's more, it's going to be a lot of fun!

These projects are designed to let children work independently as much as possible. Encourage them to do whatever they are able to do on their own. Also encourage them to try the variations when supplied and to keep a science journal. Encourage children to think like real scientists.

Before getting started, set some ground rules about using the materials and ingredients. Most important, adult supervision is a must whenever a child uses the stove, chemicals, or dry ice.

So put on your lab coats and stand by. Let your young scientists take the lead. Watch and learn. Praise their efforts. Enjoy the scientific adventure!

VISIT US AT WWW.ABDOPUBLISHING.COM

Published by ABDO Publishing Company, 8000 West 78th Street, Edina, Minnesota 55439. Copyright © 2008 by Abdo Consulting Group, Inc. International copyrights reserved in all countries. No part of this book may be reproduced in any form without written permission from the publisher. The Checkerboard Library™ is a trademark and logo of ABDO Publishing Company.

Printed in the United States.

Design and Production: Mighty Media, Inc.
Art Direction: Kelly Doudna
Photo Credits: Kelly Doudna, AbleStock, iStockphoto/Maartje van Caspel, JupiterImages Corporation, Photodisc, Shutterstock
Series Editor: Pam Price
Consultant: Scott Devens

The following manufacturers/names appearing in this book are trademarks: Fiskars, Helix, Mettler, Scotch, Sharpie, Sportline

Library of Congress Cataloging-in-Publication Data
Hopwood, James, 1964-
   Cool gravity activities : fun science projects about balance / James Hopwood.
        p. cm. -- (Cool science)
   Includes index.
   ISBN 978-1-59928-908-3
   1. Gravity--Experiments--Juvenile literature. 2. Weight (Physics)--Experiments--Juvenile literature. 3. Science projects--Juvenile literature.
I. Title.

QC178.H66 2008
531'.14078--dc22

                                                          2007010204

Contents

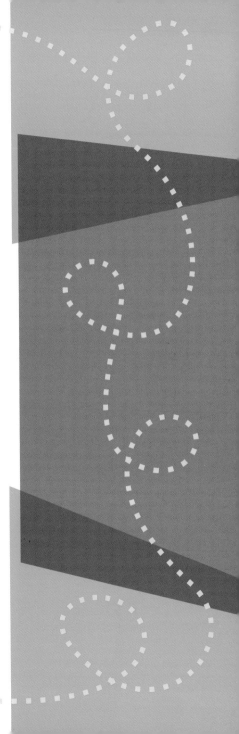

Science Is Cool

Welcome to the cool world of science! Before we get started, let's put on our thinking caps. What do the following things have in common?

- bubbles in soda pop
  - helium balloons that stay up in the air
    - sounds you hear through the headphones of your music player
      - a telescope that makes the faraway moon and stars appear closer
      - choosing your right or left eye to look through a camera viewfinder
  - your ability to balance on one foot

Did you guess that what they have in common is science? That's right, science! When you think of science, maybe you picture someone in a laboratory wearing a long white coat. Perhaps you imagine a scientist hunched over bubbling beakers and test tubes. But science is so much more. Let's take another look.

Soda pop doesn't develop bubbles until you open the container. That's because of a science called chemistry. Chemistry also explains why helium inside a balloon causes it to rise through the air.

You listen to your favorite song through the headphones attached to your music player. You look at the moon and stars through a telescope. Both activities are possible

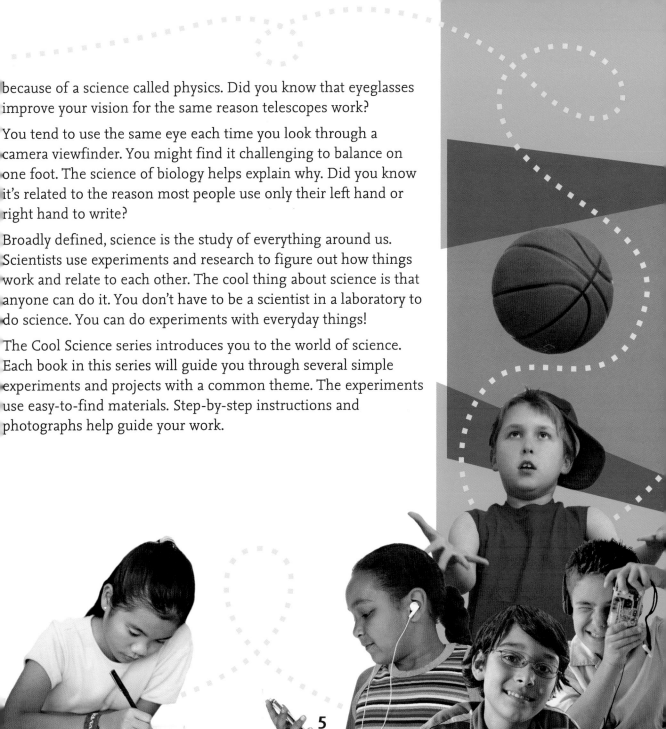

because of a science called physics. Did you know that eyeglasses improve your vision for the same reason telescopes work?

You tend to use the same eye each time you look through a camera viewfinder. You might find it challenging to balance on one foot. The science of biology helps explain why. Did you know it's related to the reason most people use only their left hand or right hand to write?

Broadly defined, science is the study of everything around us. Scientists use experiments and research to figure out how things work and relate to each other. The cool thing about science is that anyone can do it. You don't have to be a scientist in a laboratory to do science. You can do experiments with everyday things!

The Cool Science series introduces you to the world of science. Each book in this series will guide you through several simple experiments and projects with a common theme. The experiments use easy-to-find materials. Step-by-step instructions and photographs help guide your work.

The Scientific Method

Scientists have a special way of working. It is called the scientific method. The scientific method is a series of steps that a scientist follows when trying to learn something. Following the steps makes it more likely that the information you discover will be reliable.

The scientific method is described on the next page. Follow all of the steps. These steps will help you learn the best information possible. And then you can draw an accurate conclusion about what happened. You will even write notes in your own science journal, just like real scientists do!

EVEN COOLER!

Check out sections like this one throughout the book. Here you'll find instructions for variations on the project. It might be a suggestion for a different way to do the project. Or it might be a similar project that uses slightly different materials. Either way, it will make your science project even cooler!

1. Observe

Simply pay attention to something. This is called observing. A good way to prepare for the next step is to make up a what, why, or how question about what you observe. For example, let's say you observe that when you open a bottle of soda pop and pour it into a glass, it gets bubbly. Your question could be, How do bubbles get into soda?

2. Hypothesize

Think of a statement that could explain what you have observed. This statement is called a hypothesis. You might remember that you also saw bubbles in your milk when you blew into it with a straw. So your hypothesis might be, I think somebody used a straw to blow into the soda before the bottle was sealed.

3. Test

Test your hypothesis. You do this by conducting an experiment. To test your hypothesis about how bubbles get into soda, you might mix up a recipe, blow into the liquid with a straw, quickly close the container, and then open it back up.

4. Conclude

Draw a conclusion. When you do this, you tie together everything that happened in the previous steps. You report whether the result of the experiment was what you hypothesized. Perhaps there were no bubbles in your soda pop recipe when you reopened the container. You would conclude that blowing through a straw is not how fizz gets into liquids.

Write It Down

A large part of what makes science science is observation. You should observe what happens as you work through an experiment. Scientists observe everything and write notes about it in journals. You can keep a science journal too. All you need is a notebook and a pencil.

At the beginning of each activity in this book, there is a section called "Think Like a Scientist." It contains suggestions about what to record in your science journal. You can predict what you think will happen. You can write down what did happen. And you can draw a conclusion, especially if what really happened is different from what you predicted.

As you do experiments, record things in your journal. You will be working just like a real scientist!

THINK LIKE A SCIENTIST!
Look for a box like this one on the first page of each project. It will give you ideas about what to write in your science journal before, during, and after your experiments. There may be questions about the project. There may be a suggestion about how to look at the project in a different way. Your science journal is the place to keep track of everything!

EVEN COOLER!
You can record more than just words in your journal. You can sketch pictures and make charts. If you have a camera, you can even add photos to your journal!

Safe Science

Good scientists practice safe science. Here are some important things to remember.

- Check with an adult before you begin any project. Sometimes you'll need an adult to buy materials or help you handle them for a while. For some projects, an adult will need to help you the whole time. The instructions will say when an adult should assist you.

- Ask for help if you're unsure about how to do something.

- If you or someone else is hurt, tell an adult immediately.

- Read the list of things you'll need. Gather everything before you begin working on a project.

- Don't taste, eat, or drink any of the materials or the results unless the directions say that you can.

- Use protective gear. Scientists wear safety goggles to protect their eyes. They wear gloves to protect their hands from chemicals and possible burns. They wear aprons or lab coats to protect their clothing.

- Clean up when you are finished. That includes putting away materials and washing containers, work surfaces, and your hands.

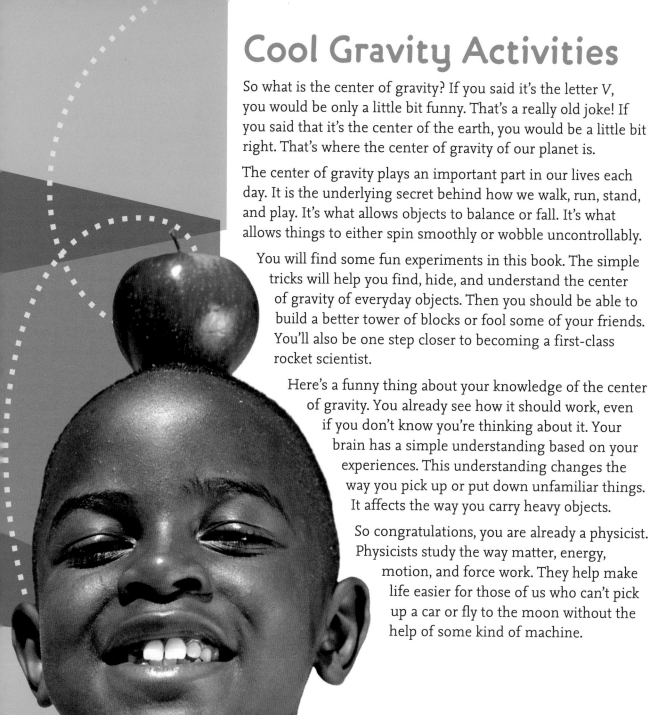

Cool Gravity Activities

So what is the center of gravity? If you said it's the letter V, you would be only a little bit funny. That's a really old joke! If you said that it's the center of the earth, you would be a little bit right. That's where the center of gravity of our planet is.

The center of gravity plays an important part in our lives each day. It is the underlying secret behind how we walk, run, stand, and play. It's what allows objects to balance or fall. It's what allows things to either spin smoothly or wobble uncontrollably.

You will find some fun experiments in this book. The simple tricks will help you find, hide, and understand the center of gravity of everyday objects. Then you should be able to build a better tower of blocks or fool some of your friends. You'll also be one step closer to becoming a first-class rocket scientist.

Here's a funny thing about your knowledge of the center of gravity. You already see how it should work, even if you don't know you're thinking about it. Your brain has a simple understanding based on your experiences. This understanding changes the way you pick up or put down unfamiliar things. It affects the way you carry heavy objects.

So congratulations, you are already a physicist. Physicists study the way matter, energy, motion, and force work. They help make life easier for those of us who can't pick up a car or fly to the moon without the help of some kind of machine.

The center of gravity is the center of an object's mass. We'll call it the center of gravity because we will be working with the gravity of the earth.

The center of gravity is the exact point on which an object will balance perfectly. That point is not always the center of an object though. Sometimes an object has a center of gravity that is near one end. Sometimes the center of gravity is even outside of the object!

Astronauts use what they know about the center of gravity to avoid tumbling wildly when they work in space. But understanding the center of gravity has everyday uses too. You'll know if an object will move or spin when you apply force to it. You'll know if something will stand up, balance, or tumble to the ground. You'll even be able to fool your friends into believing they can do something impossible!

What you do with what you learn is entirely up to you. But, it's always a good idea to have fun when you learn. So let's get started!

Materials

You can probably find these supplies around the house.

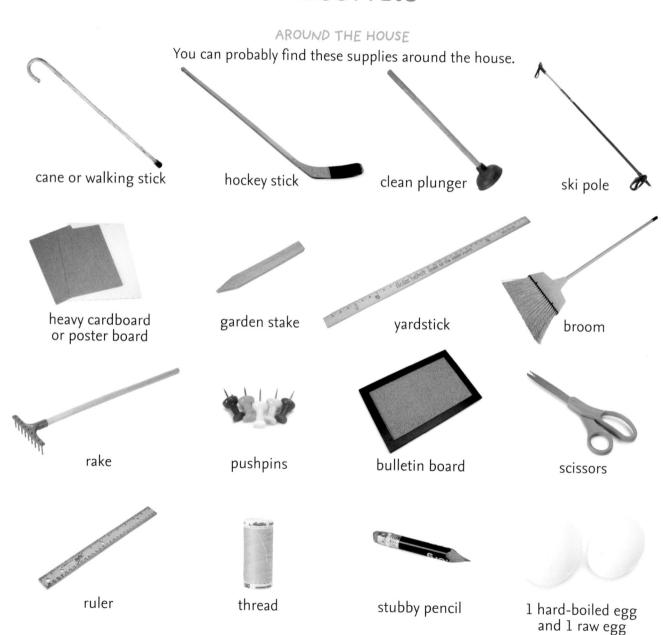

cane or walking stick

hockey stick

clean plunger

ski pole

heavy cardboard
or poster board

garden stake

yardstick

broom

rake

pushpins

bulletin board

scissors

ruler

thread

stubby pencil

1 hard-boiled egg
and 1 raw egg

12

tape

stopwatch

soda straw

3 × 5 index cards

straight pins

2 equal-size blocks

paper punch

8½ × 11 paper

poster board
or file folder

hot-glue gun

color markers

craft stick or
wooden coffee stir stick

2 metal forks

AT THE HARDWARE STORE
You can find these supplies at a hardware store.

straight handle
or dowel

heavy metal washers

13

The Old Cane Trick

TIME: ABOUT 10 MINUTES

MATERIALS

cane or walking stick

hockey stick

clean plunger

ski pole

rake

garden stake

yardstick

broom

straight handle or dowel

PHYSICS

You can make the balance point of a long object reveal itself. Try an **asymmetrical** object such as a plunger. Try a **symmetrical** object such as a yardstick. This trick works every time!

THINK LIKE A SCIENTIST!

Write your thoughts about the following in your science journal.

1. Sketch each object. Draw an arrow pointing to where you predict the center of gravity will be.

2. When you're finished, draw an arrow pointing to where the center of gravity really is.

3. Why were your predictions right or wrong?

4. Which object was the easiest to balance? Which object was the most difficult? Why?

1. Pick up the first test object and hold it horizontally in front of you. Place your hands toward the ends of the item and turn them so your thumbs are pointing up. The object should rest on your index fingers.

2. Slowly move your hands together, keeping the object level. You may have to move one hand more than the other. Observe how the weight of the object feels as you move your hands.

3. When your hands come together, you should find that the object is balanced on top of your hands. Now gently pull away one hand and slightly roll the other hand. Your test object should be balanced on one finger.

4. Repeat the experiment with each of your test objects. Before you start, try to guess where the balance point is.

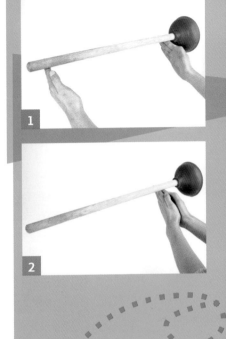

The Science behind the Fun

With your hands far apart, the weight of the object is distributed almost equally on each hand. Each hand acts as a **fulcrum**, or pivot point, like the one in a seesaw. As each hand moves toward the center of balance, it holds more of the total weight than it did before. Finally, your hands meet at the point where all the weight is supported in one spot. This spot is as close to the object's center of gravity as your hands can get.

Science at Work

When you lift or carry something long, it is easiest to hold it at a balance point. Your energy goes mostly to support the load. And, you don't waste energy trying to keep your load from tipping. If you can't get a grip at a balance point on something big and tippy, get a second person to help you carry it. Long objects are less tippy when the center of gravity is suspended between two supports.

Tops Don't Have to Be Round

TIME: ABOUT 30 MINUTES

The center of gravity is the center of balance. That also makes it the center of spin. In this activity, you will build a fun twirling device.

MATERIALS

heavy cardboard or poster board

pushpins

bulletin board

scissors

ruler

thread, about 1 yard

heavy metal washer

stubby pencil

tape

PHYSICS

THINK LIKE A SCIENTIST!

Write about these topics in your science journal.

1. How did you decide where to predict the center of gravity?
2. Was the center of gravity where you predicted it would be?
3. What kind of line did the top draw when you spun it? Why do you think it drew this line?

16

1. Draw a lumpy shape about five inches across on the poster board. Cut the shape out. Draw a small X where you think the center of gravity is on your shape.

2. Use a pushpin to make five holes around the edge of your shape. Wiggle the pin in each hole to slightly enlarge it.

3. Tie one end of the thread to the pushpin and one end to the **washer**. The weight will hang down and act as a **plumb bob**.

4. Now slip the pin with the thread and washer through one of the holes in the shape. Loosely pin the shape to the bulletin board. Let the shape hang down from the pin. Wait for the washer to stop moving and hang straight down again.

The Science behind the Fun

When you hang an object, it will turn until its center of gravity is directly below the suspension point. Here, the pin supports the full weight of the object. The object stops moving when it reaches a state of balance. At that point, the center of gravity is vertically aligned with the pin. Each time you change the suspension point, you see a new vertical line that the center of gravity must lie on. The center of gravity is also the center of mass. That makes it the exact point on which an object will spin freely.

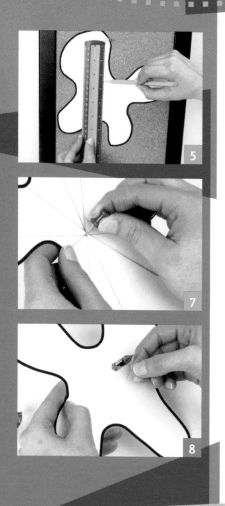

5 Mark the line where the thread crosses the shape. Place the ruler's edge against the pin and hold it along the thread. Be careful not to move the thread or the shape. Trace the thread line onto the shape.

6 Repeat steps 4 and 5 for each hole you made. Remove the shape from the bulletin board when you finish marking the last line.

7 All five lines should cross in one spot. Push a pin through the spot where they cross to make a starter hole. This is the center of gravity on your shape.

8 Carefully push the pencil stub through the pin hole. Tape the tiny torn edges to the pencil to hold the shape in place.

9 Spin your new top on a piece of paper and watch how it moves. Check out what kind of line it leaves behind.

10 Try finding the center of gravity of other, more unlikely shapes. Try a **crescent**, a cane, or a doughnut shape.

Science at Work

When using a crane, construction workers connect the cable directly over the load's center of gravity. Otherwise, when the crane lifts the load, it will swing until it reaches a point of balance. Recall how your shape swung when you pinned it to the board. That motion can be dangerous if it involves a heavy load!

Science for Breakfast

TIME: ABOUT 25 MINUTES

MATERIALS
1 raw egg
1 hard-boiled egg
stopwatch

PHYSICS

Now that you have an idea of how the center of gravity affects balance and spin, let's see how your brain can be fooled by your eyes.

THINK LIKE A SCIENTIST!
Complete the chart in your science journal. Then answer these questions.
1. What does your data tell you?
2. What unexpected result surprised you?
3. Explain why you think the surprise happened.
4. How can you prove your theory?

1
Create a data chart like this one in your science journal. In it, you will record how long a raw egg and a hard-boiled egg rotate when you spin them.

	Cooked egg	Uncooked egg
Spin 1		
Spin 2		
Spin 3		

2
Place the raw egg on a table and spin it. Time how long the egg spins. This experiment works best if the same person spins the egg the same way each time. If a spin doesn't start out right, try it again. This is an experiment, not a spinning contest!

3
Watch carefully as the egg spins. Note whether it moves smoothly or wobbles. Don't let your egg fall and break. Not only is it messy but you will lose all your test data! If the egg gets too close to the edge, stop it and time a new spin.

4
When the egg stops spinning, record the spin time. Also note your observations of the egg's behavior.

5
Repeat steps 2 through 4 two more times with the raw egg. Then do the experiment three times with the hard-boiled egg.

The Science behind the Fun

In an uncooked egg, the yolk is more **dense** than the white. As the egg spins, the yolk moves around, changing the egg's center of gravity. This means it keeps changing the axis on which the egg will spin, making it lose energy with each change. That energy loss slows the egg to a stop faster.

However, the inside of a hard-boiled egg is solid. Its center of gravity doesn't change when you spin it. Its spin is more stable, and it loses less energy to wobbles and **friction**. This gives it longer and more impressive spins.

EVEN COOLER!

Conduct the egg-spinning experiment again. But this time, try spinning the eggs on their ends instead of their sides.

Science at Work

An unstable mass makes for an unstable center of gravity. This can cause moving objects to quickly tumble out of control. For example, if the items in a box fall to one side, the box might seem to jump from your hands. In the shipping business, that is called a shifting load. When you need to control a container, be sure the things inside cannot move around, or you may be surprised by an unexpected imbalance.

Balance and Leverage

TIME: ABOUT 45 MINUTES

MATERIALS
soda straw
ruler
3 × 5 index cards
straight pin
two equal-size blocks that are shorter than the straw
scissors
paper punch

In this experiment, you will see how **leverage** and shape can also affect an object's center of gravity.

PHYSICS

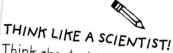

THINK LIKE A SCIENTIST!

Think about what you observed in this experiment. Then answer these questions in your science journal.

1. How could you balance two objects that are not the same length?

2. If the straw you used is bendable, how does the extra plastic on one end affect the center of gravity of the balance arm?

3. What happens if you attach the long pan by the long side instead of the short side?

22

1 Measure the length of the straw and mark its center point. Also mark points one inch from each end of the straw.

2 Fold one index card in half crosswise and cut it along the fold. These are your short pans. Fold the second card in half lengthwise and cut it along the fold. These are your long pans.

3 Use scissors to cut a slit in each end of the straw up to the inch marks. Make sure the slits line up. Insert one short pan into each slit.

4 With the pans lying flat, push a straight pin through the upper half of the straw at the center point. This is the **fulcrum** of your balance arm. Stack the blocks and place the pin between them.

Science at Work

Some chairs have a seat that extends past the legs a little bit. That's fine, unless someone uses the chair as a step stool. Let's say someone stood on that overhang and put a toe on the back of the chair for balance. It might feel safe, but it isn't.

Leverage is what allows that little bit of weight on the chair back to counterbalance the large weight on the overhang. If that toe slipped off the back of the chair, the weight on the overhang would suddenly tip the chair. That is why step stools have a base that is wider than the part you stand on.

5 If the scale is not level, slide the pan on the high side outward a little bit until the balance is level. Note how this adjustment works.

6 Use a paper punch to make about 20 dots from another index card.

7 Balance the scale with a long pan resting on each of the short pans and notice their final positions. They should be about equal distance from the center.

8 Now remove the long pans. Replace one of the short pans with one of the long pans. Insert the short side of the long pan in the slit. Watch what happens to the balance.

9 Add some dots to the short pan until the two sides are level again. Notice how many it takes.

The Science behind the Fun

Two principles are at work here, center of gravity and **leverage**. The balance arm you made is a lever, and the pin is the **fulcrum**. As one side of the lever got longer, it gained more leverage than the shorter side. So even though the long pan and the short pan weigh the same, the side with the long pan has more leverage. The force of gravity pulling on it overcame the short end, so you had to add mass to the short pan to balance the scale.

Amazing Acrobatics

TIME: ABOUT 45 MINUTES

MATERIALS

8½ × 11 paper

poster board
or file folder

ruler

2 heavy metal
washers

tape or hot glue

color markers

PHYSICS

Build an amazing acrobat
that will fool your eyes. See how
density and size can make you think
you see something that you don't.

THINK LIKE A SCIENTIST!

Write your answers to these
questions in your science journal.

1. Did your figure work as
   expected? If not, why not?
   How could you change the
   design to make it work?

2. Can you design a balancing
   figure that uses a single
   counterweight? Sketch it in
   your science journal. Be sure
   to show the balance point and
   where the counterweight goes.

1 Fold a sheet of paper in half lengthwise, then open it back up to create a centerline. Draw an inch-wide (2.5 cm) circle in each of the two bottom corners. They should almost touch the paper's edges. This is where the counterweights will go.

2 Draw a quarter-inch (0.6 cm) circle on the fold about four inches (10 cm) from the bottom of the page. This will be the balance point.

3 Now draw an acrobatic figure on the paper like the one shown here. Try to fill the whole sheet. Don't make any part too skinny to stand up on its own. Make sure that your design goes all the way to the circles in the lower corners. You don't want to cut away the hiding spots for your counterweights!

4 Position the paper with your artwork on the poster board. Tack it down with a few small pieces of tape. Then cut out the figure.

The Science behind the Fun

A longer or larger portion of an object looks like it would have more **leverage** on the balance point than a smaller one. That's the secret to this optical illusion. What keeps the acrobat upright is the heavy washers. They have a much higher **density** than the paper. So, they hide a large amount of mass in a small area. Because the washers weigh more than the rest of the figure, the center of gravity lies below the balance point and between the counterweights.

5 Use tape or hot glue to attach the heavy **washers** to the back of the posterboard figure. Make sure they are behind the circles you drew in step 1.

6 Place your fingertip under the balance point. The figure should stay upright, even though it looks like it should fall over. If your figure doesn't stand up, the counterweights are probably not heavy enough. Add more weight to the counterweights.

7 When your figure is working, go ahead and decorate it. You know you want to!

Science at Work

Did you ever wonder why a crane's long arm doesn't pull the crane over? Perhaps you've wondered how a forklift can pick up a heavy load without tipping forward. Well, the answer is attached to your acrobat. Those heavy lifters have massive steel counterweights hidden in the back. Without that large amount of **deadweight** built into the machines, they couldn't do their jobs at all.

EVEN COOLER!

Use more paper or poster board to hide the washers on the back. Then you can decorate both sides so the figure can be seen from the front and the back without revealing the trick. To display your acrobat, first cut a small notch under the balance point. Attach the ends of a string to two points in your room. Set the notch on the string. The acrobat will balance on the tightrope!

Flying Forks for Fun

TIME: ABOUT 3 MINUTES

MATERIALS

craft stick or wooden coffee stir stick about 5 inches long

two metal forks

PHYSICS

You can do this demonstration for your family at dinner.

THINK LIKE A SCIENTIST!

Answer these questions in your science journal.

1. Try changing the width of the V that the forks make. How does that affect the overall center of gravity?

2. Is it easier to balance the forks when they make a wider V or narrower V? Why do you think that is?

1 Pick up the craft stick, find its center of gravity, and balance it on your finger. Tell your family that you have now found its center of gravity.

2 Now tell them that the center of gravity is a powerful force. By knowing exactly where it is, you can hang two forks off one end of the stick and it will still balance. This is not really true, so be ready for your family to argue.

3 Cross the tines of the two forks to form a V. Lay the forks on the table. Push the tip of the stick through the crossed tines. The forks and the stick must be securely wedged together so they don't wiggle around. The handles of the fork need to hang lower than the stick.

4 Now put your finger under the center of the stick as before. Balance the whole arrangement on your finger.

5 This is a science trick and not a magic trick. So, you can tell your family why the forks balance and let them try it.

EVEN COOLER!
Break the stick at the balance point. Then you can hang the flying forks from the edge of a glass. That looks pretty weird to people who don't understand how it balances!

Science at Work
Magicians use the principles of **leverage** and center of gravity to fool human **perception**. That's how they make heavy things look light and light things look heavy. It's how they make objects seem to appear, fly, and vanish. They also will tell a story that leads you to believe something that is not true. Just like saying, "It's the stick's center of gravity that does the balancing."

The Science behind the Fun
In this case, the weight of the stick is insignificant compared with the weight of the forks. Remember, the center of gravity determines the balance point. In this trick, it usually lies about two and a half inches (13 cm) from the point where the forks meet. The stick lets you support the structure at its balance point. Without the stick, the center of gravity for the forks would be in empty air.

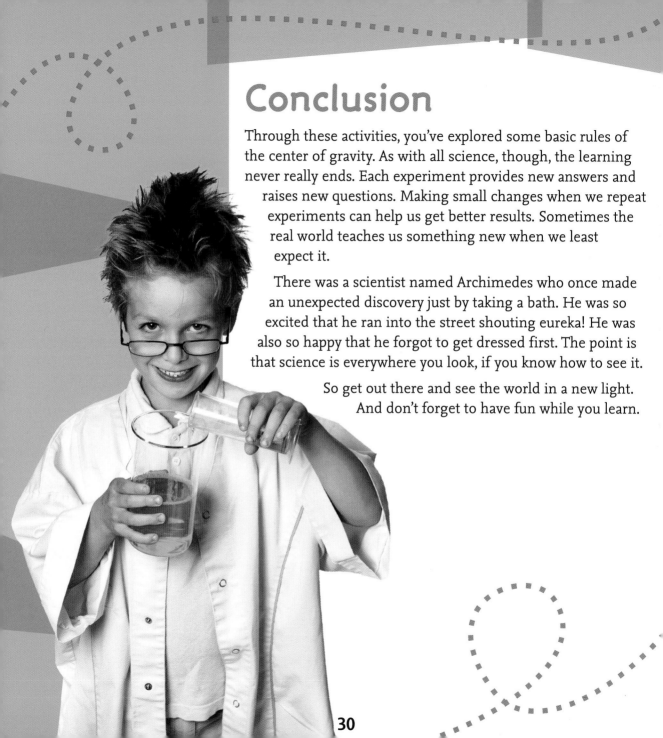

Conclusion

Through these activities, you've explored some basic rules of the center of gravity. As with all science, though, the learning never really ends. Each experiment provides new answers and raises new questions. Making small changes when we repeat experiments can help us get better results. Sometimes the real world teaches us something new when we least expect it.

There was a scientist named Archimedes who once made an unexpected discovery just by taking a bath. He was so excited that he ran into the street shouting eureka! He was also so happy that he forgot to get dressed first. The point is that science is everywhere you look, if you know how to see it.

So get out there and see the world in a new light. And don't forget to have fun while you learn.

Glossary

asymmetrical – when parts on either side of a centerline are not alike.

crescent – shaped like the moon in its first or last quarter, with less than half being visible.

deadweight – the weight of an object that is not moving.

dense – in physics, having a high mass in a small volume.

density – in physics, the quantity or mass of a substance per unit of volume.

friction – the rubbing of one surface or object against another.

fulcrum – the support on which a lever turns.

leverage – force or power gained by using a lever, such as a crowbar.

perception – the act of using senses such as sight or hearing to gather information about one's surroundings.

plumb bob – a weight attached to a plumb line, which is used to find a vertical line.

symmetrical – having two sides that are identical to each other.

washer – a flat ring that is used to make a joint tight, reduce friction, or prevent a leak.

WEB SITES

To learn more about the the center of gravity, visit ABDO Publishing Company on the World Wide Web at **www.abdopublishing. com.** Web sites about the center of gravity are featured on our Book Links page. These links are routinely monitored and updated to provide the most current information available.

Index